The month of July, from the illuminated manuscript
Les Très Riches Heures du duc de Berry

The Story of a Special Day
Volume 186

July

4

185th day of the year
(186th in leap years)
180 days remaining
until the end of the year.

by Michael Dobson

Timespinner Press

Table of Contents

Cover: Fourth of July fireworks in Washington, DC — for the *Event of the Day.*

Back Cover and Frontispiece: The month of July, from the French Gothic illuminated manuscript *Les Très Riches Heures du duc de Berry.*

July 4 Quotations

One never notices what has been done; one can only see what remains to be done.

> — *Marie Curie, died July 4, 1934*

Rose-colored glasses are never made in bifocals. Nobody wants to read the small print in dreams.

> — *Ann Landers, born July 4, 1918*

Nothing in the world can take the place of persistence. Talent will not; nothing is more common than unsuccessful men with talent. Genius will not; unrewarded genius is almost a proverb. Education will not; the world is full of educated derelicts. Persistence and determination alone are omnipotent. The slogan "press on" has solved and always will solve the problems of the human race.

> — *Calvin Coolidge, born July 4, 1872*

I must study politics and war, that our sons may have liberty to study mathematics and philosophy.

> — *John Adams, died July 4, 1826*

There is no act, however virtuous, for which ingenuity may not find some bad motive.

> — *Thomas Jefferson, died July 4, 1826*

Nobody, I think, ought to read poetry, or look at pictures or statues, who cannot find a great deal more in them than the poet or artist has actually expressed.

> — *Nathaniel Hawthorne, born July 4, 1804*

Event of the Day
American Independence Day

The US Declaration of Independence

Quick — what day did the Thirteen Colonies declare their independence from Great Britain? The answer isn't what you probably think. The Continental Congress unanimously approved the independence resolution on July 2, 1776. It was two days later, on July 4, that the Congress got around to passing the official announcement in the form of the United States Declaration of Independence.

No less than John Adams, author of the preamble ("When in the course of human events...") and subsequently third President of the United States, urged that July 2, not 4, be celebrated. He wrote,

> "The second day of July, 1776, will be the most memorable epocha in the history of America. I am apt to believe that it will be celebrated by succeeding generations as the great anniversary festival. It ought to be

commemorated as the day of deliverance, by solemn acts of devotion to God Almighty. It ought to be solemnized with pomp and parade, with shows, games, sports, guns, bells, bonfires, and illuminations, from one end of this continent to the other, from this time forward forevermore."

Adams notwithstanding, popular sentiment quickly established the ratification of the Declaration of Independence on July 4 as America's national birthday. (Although the Declaration was passed on July 4, it wasn't actually signed until August 2.)

By the time the Declaration of Independence passed, the Thirteen Colonies and Great Britain had already been at war for more than a year. After increasing tumult and civil unrest dating back to 1763, the first actual military engagement of the war came on April 19, 1775, in the Battles of Lexington and Concord, both in Massachusetts, ending in American victory in both battles.

There was still substantial sentiment in the Colonies for reconciliation with Great Britain. A Second Continental Congress began meeting in Philadelphia in May 1775. (The First Continental Congress the previous year had only established a boycott of British goods and a petition to King George III.)

The Second Continental Congress was far from unanimous in wanting independence. Most would have been satisfied by some concessions from the British government, but George III and his advisors were in no mood to placate the unruly colonists.

"Writing the Declaration of Independence 1776," by Jean Leon Gerome Ferris. (from left to right: Benjamin Franklin, John Adams, Thomas Jefferson

In fact, most colonial delegations had no authority to vote for independence, and many delegates had to lobby their own states for permission. The first part of the Declaration of Independence, the preamble authored by John Adams, was passed on May 15, with four colonies voting against it.

On June 11, Congress authorized a "Committee of Five": John Adams, Benjamin Franklin, Thomas Jefferson, New York's Robert Livingston, and Connecticut's Roger Sherman to draft a full declaration. Jefferson wrote the first draft, modified it based on input from the other four, and on June 28, the Declaration of Independence moved to the floor of Congress. Formal debate began on July 1, and the following day independence was approved.

There was a lot of editing left to do, and Congress cut about a fourth from the committee's draft, and on July 4, 1776, the Declaration of Independence was approved and sent to the printer.

American Independence Day, more commonly called simply the Fourth of July, is celebrated with fireworks, parades, concerts, baseball games, and political ceremonies.

As a midsummer holiday, it's also an occasion for barbecues and family reunions. Because of the extra holiday, the first week of July is one of the busiest travel periods of the year.

John Adams and Thomas Jefferson, who were the only signers of the Declaration to later serve as president, both died on the Fourth of July, 1826, the fiftieth anniversary of American independence.

July 4 Holidays and Celebrations

Arag ng Kalayaan (Philippines)

On July 4, 1946, the Phillipines, which had been a US territory since 1898, became the fully independent Republic of the Philippines. Filipino-American Friendship Day (previously called Republic Day) is celebrated each year on July 4.

Liberation Day (Rwanda)

The African nation of Rwanda marks the end of the Rwandan genocide, which killed at least 500,000 people, as Liberation Day each July 4.

Christian Feast Days

In **Western Christianity**, July 4 is the feast day of Andrew of Crete, Bertha of Artois, Blessed Catherine Jarrige, Blessed Pier Giorgio Frassati, Elizabeth of Portugal, Oda of Canterbury, and Ulrich of Augsburg.

In **Eastern Orthodox Christianity**, May 28 is the feast of Andrew of Crete, Venerable Martha, Theodore of Cyrene, Andrei Rublev, the family of Tsar Nicholas II, and Prince Andrew I Bogolyubsky. (These events are observed on July 17 by "Old Calendarists.")

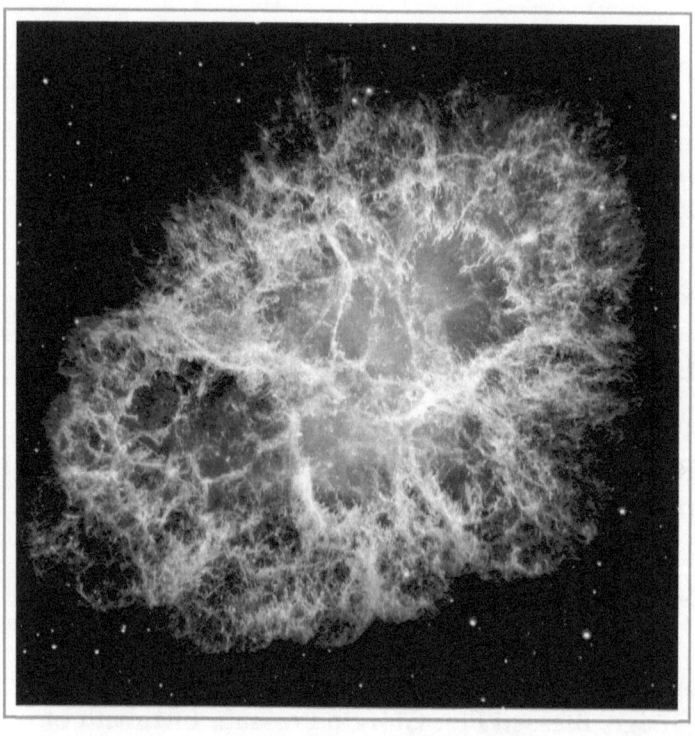

The Crab Nebula, photographed by the Hubble Space Telescope

What Happened on July 4?

1054 CE – **Light from the Crab Nebula Supernova Reaches Earth**

On July 4, 1054, Chinese astronomers recorded the appearance of a "guest star" in the heavens that blazed so brightly it could be seen in broad daylight for 23 days and prominently in the night sky for about two years. Later records from 13th century Japan also mention the event; there are some less certain references from Europe in the 15th century and even a Native American petroglyph.

Known to astronomers as SN 1054 (the "SN" stands for "Supernova") this titanic event released as much energy in a few weeks as our Sun is expected to emit over its entire lifetime. Today, the remnants of that tremendous explosion are known as the Crab Nebula (left), which has expanded to cover 11 light years and is still expanding at a rate of 1,500 kilometers per second. At its center is the Crab Pulsar, a neutron star, which is still the strongest emitter of X-ray and gamma ray energy in the galaxy.

The Crab Nebula is approximately 6,500 light years from Earth, or 1,625 times as far away as the closest star to our Solar System.

Portrait of George Washington by Charles Wilson Peale

This is the oldest authenticated portrait of George Washington, showing him in his colonel's uniform. It was painted in 1772, after the French and Indian War but before the American Revolution.

1744 CE – **Treaty of Lancaster**

Beginning on June 25, 1744, and concluding on July 4, 1744, representatives of the Iroquois Six Nations and the colonies of Virginia and Maryland, meetig in Lancaster, Pennsylvania, renegotiated the boundary between the Iroquois and the colonists. It ended with the Iroquois agreeing to sell their claim to the Shenandoah Valley for £200. Each side interpreted the agreement diferently: the Iroquois thought they had only ceded the Shenandoah Valley, and the Virginians believed that they had rights to all the land as far as the Pacific, a contributing cause to the French and Indian War.

1754 CE – **George Washington Surrenders**

Lt. Col. George Washington of the Virginia colonial militia fought one of the first engagements of what evolved into the French and Indian War when he engaged French troops in the Battle of Jumonville Glen. Washington was accused by the French of ordering a massacre of surrendered forces (historians differ), including the French commander.

Expecting pursuit, Washington and his forces built a fort he named Fort Necessity, a circular stockade made of logs with a small hut in the center.

After a small battle, the outnumbered Washington surrendered, signing a document in French that, among other things, stated that the French commander had been "assasinated." The Fort Necessity National Battlefield in Fayette County, Pennsylvania, marks the site.

1825 CE – **Erie Canal Construction Begins**

The 353 mile long Erie Canal, linking the Hudson River at Albany, New York, to Lake Erie at Buffalo, New York, began construction on July 4, 1817, opening eight years later on October 26, 1825. The canal, one of the most important public works projects in US history, created a navigable water route from the Atlantic Ocean to the Great Lakes, cutting transport costs by 95%. It was replaced in 1918 by the larger New York State Barge Canal, but still carries some traffic.

The Erie Canal by W. H. Bartlett, 1839.

1831 CE – **"My Country, 'Tis of Thee"**

Samuel Francis Smith wrote "My Country, 'Tis of Thee," using the same tune as the British "God Save the Queen." The song was first performed publicly during the 1831 Boston Fourth of July festivities.

1855 CE – *Leaves of Grass*

One of the major works of American poetry, Walt Whitman's *Leaves of Grass* was first published on July 4, 1855.

1862 CE – **Lewis Carroll Tells a Story**

On July 4, 1862, Rev. Charles L. Dodgson rowed up the Thames with another pastor and the three young daughters of Henry Lidell. During the trip, Dodgson made up a story about a bored little girl named Alice who goes looking for adventure. Alice Liddell begged Dodgson to write down the story, which became *Alice's Adventures in Wonderland*, published under Dodgson's literary pseudonym, Lewis Carroll.

Alice with the Rabbit and the Mad Hatter, by John Tenniel

1863 CE – **Vicksburg Surrenders to Grant**

After a siege lasting more than forty days, the Confederate fortress city of Vicksburg, Mississippi, surrendered to Union forces commanded by Gen. Ulysses S. Grant on July 4, 1863, completing the Vicksburg Campaign.

1863 CE – **Lee Retreats from Gettysburg**

Following a terrible three day battle that raged from July 1 to July 3, Confederate Gen. Robert E. Lee began the retreat from Gettysburg on July 4, 1863. A lack of aggressive pursuit by Union forces allowed it to withdraw successfully across the Potomac River.

1879 CE – **Anglo-Zulu War Ends**

After delivering an insulting ultimatum to Zulu King Cetshwayo to provoke war, the British invaded the Zulu Kingdom in early 1879. Famous for the Zulu victory at the Battle of Isandlwana and for the brave British defense at Rorke's Drift, superior British firepower at the Battle of Ulundi, July 4, 1879, resulted in the final defeat of the Zulu and the loss of their independence.

1881 CE – **Tuskegee Institute Opens**

Founded by African-American educator Booker T. Washington on July 4, 1881, the Tuskegee Institute is one of the earliest and most famous historically black universities in America, and is now a National Historic Landmark.

1892 CE – **Western Samoa Has Two Fourths of July**

On July 4, 1892, after urging from traders, the King of Samoa moved his small Pacific island nation to the other side of the then-unofficial International Date Line, meaning that the day after July 4 was also July 4, and Western Samoa had a 367-day year.

1894 CE – **Republic of Hawaii Proclaimed**

After foreign business interests, assisted by the US military, overthrew the Kingdom of Hawaii in 1893, the provisional leaders of the Pacific nation proclaimed the Republic of Hawaii on July 4, 1894. The short-lived republic was annexed by the United States on July 7, 1898.

1902 CE – **Philippine-American War Ends**

Following the Spanish-American War, the Philippines declared their independence from Spain, only to be annexed by United States in 1898. This triggerd the Philippine-American War (Digmaang Pilipino-Amerikano), which raged from 1899 to 1902. Estimates of Filipino civilians killed in the conflict range from 200,000 to 1.5 million; about 4,000 American soldiers died. Although the Philippines formally capitulated on July 4, 1902, resistance groups continued fighting for as much as a decade. The Philippines remained an American colony until after World War II, finally achieving independence on July 4, 1946.

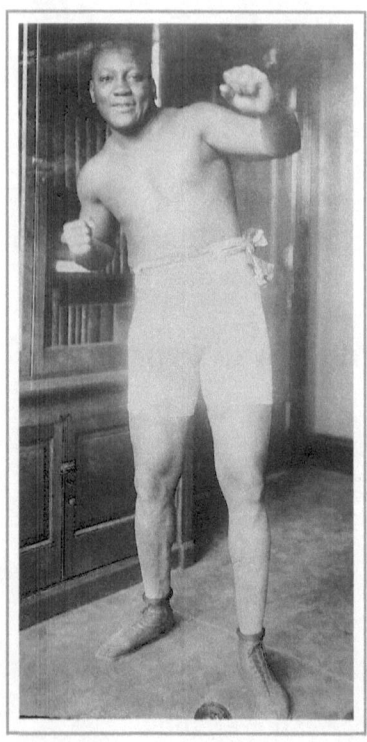

1910 CE – **"Fight of the Century"**

Boxer Jack Johnson (left), known as the Galveston Giant, was the first African American world heavyweight champion.

Racial animosity from whites led to calls for a "Great White Hope" to retrieve the title from Johnson. Retired undefeated heavyweight champion James Jeffries faced Johnson on July 4, 1910 in Reno, Nevada, and lost badly. Numerous black celebrations were termed "race riots," resulting in attacks from angry white citizens. Eight blacks and five whites died, along with hundreds of injuries. A film of the match was banned in America.

Johnson kept the title for five years, finally losing to white boxer Jess Willard. In later life he founded what became known as the Cotton Club, and after being sent to prison for consorting with a white woman, inented a new form of wrench, for which he received US Patent 1,413,121.

1927 CE – **Lockheed Vega Takes Flight**

The Lockheed Vega, a six passenger monoplane, first took flight on July 4, 1927. The plane was used by Amelia Earhart in her solo flight across the Atlantic and by Wiley Post for his around-the-world flight. Both Vegas are in the collection of the Smithsonian Institution's National Air and Space Museum.

1939 CE – **Lou Gehrig Retires**

Known as the "Iron Horse," baseball great Lou Gehrig (right) was diagnosed with amyotrophic lateral sclerosis, often called Lou Gehrig's disease. In an Independence Day double-header, the New York Yankees celebrated "Lou Gehrig Appreciation Day," and accorded him the honor of being the first player in Major League Baseball to have his uniform number retired. In a speech on the occasion, Gehrig called himself "the luckiest man on the face of the earth." He was elected to the Baseball Hall of Fame the same year, and died in 1941.

1950 CE – **Radio Free Europe Goes On the Air**

Founded to provide news, information, and entertainment to countries "where the free flow of information is either banned by government authorities or not fully developed," Radio Free Europe began broadcasting on July 4, 1950. Numerous attempts were made to jam its signals and infiltrate its staff, but Radio Free Europe and its sister network Radio Liberty, aimed at the Soviet Union, gained a reputation as one of the most reliable sources of news behind the Iron Curtain.

1960 CE – **50-Star American Flag**

After the admission of Hawaii and Alaska as states in 1959, the 48-star flag of the United States was replaced by a new 50-star flag, which first flew in Philadelphia on July 4, 1960.

1976 CE – **Raid on Entebbe**

Following the June 27 hijacking of an Air France Airbus A300, the Palestinian and German revolutionary groups threatened to kill the more than 100 Israeli and Jewish passengers if their demands were not met. In response, on July 4, 1976, commandos of the Israel Defense Force made a daring nighttime rescue raid on Entebbe, Uganda, where the plane was located. One commando was killed, along with three hostages. All the hijackers were killed, along with 45 Ugandan soldiers and 30 Ugandan Air Force MiG fighters.

1987 CE – **Klaus Barbie Convicted**

Known as the "Butcher of Lyon," Gestapo officer Klaus Barbie was extradited from Bolivia, tried in a French court, and on July 4, 1987, was sentenced to life imprisonment. He died four years later.

1997 CE – **Pathfinder Lands on Mars**

Launched December 4, 1996, the NASA Mars Pathfinder landed on July 4, 1997 on the red planet. Its robotic rover carried out numerous experiments to gain knowledge of the Martian environment. Although the mission was only scheduled to last a month, Pathfinder operated for almost three months, finally failing on September 27, 1997.

The Pathfinder rover on the surface of Mars

2005 CE – **Deep Impact Hits a Comet**

The NASA Deep Impact space probe was designed
to study the composition of comets. Launched
January 12, 2005, it intercepted comet 9P/Tempel
and released an impactor that collided with the
nucleus of the comet on July 4, 2005, returning the
first information about the interior of a comet. It was
then retasked for an extended mission to explore
other comets, and as of 2013 is still operational.

2012 CE – **Higgs Boson Discovered**

In 1964, Peter Higgs, along with other physicists,
suggested that a hitherto undiscovered subatomic
particle was needed to explain some of the elements
of the Standard Model of physics. The Higgs boson,
as it was called, was so important to the
understanding of fundamental physics that a 40 year
search for the particle took place. The Large Hadron
Collider at Cern, Switzerland, was built in part to
aid the search for the Higgs boson. On July 4, 2012, a
new particle with the predicted characteristics was
found, and has been tentatively identified as the
elusive boson. Research continues into its properties.

Who Was Born on July 4?

Animals

Koko (July 4, 1971 —)

Gorilla Koko can understand over 1,000 signs based on American Sign Language and around 2,000 words of spoken English. Her name is short for Hanabiko (花火子) or "fireworks child," for her birthday.

Business

Richard Garriott (July 4, 1961 —)

Well-known video game developer Richard (Lord British) Garriott created the Ultima computer game series. He flew to the International Space Station as a tourist in 2008.

Michael Milken (July 4, 1946 —)

Financier Michael Milken served two years for insider trading in a highly publicized 1989 case.

Leona Helmsley (July 4, 1920 — August 20, 2007)

Hotel and real estate magnate Leona Helmsley became known as the "Queen of Mean" for her abrasive management style. She served 16 months for tax evasion, and is associated with a statement reported by a former housekeeper: "We don't pay taxes. Only little people pay taxes."

James Bailey (July 4, 1847 — April 11, 1906)

Circus ringmaster James Bailey (left)partnered with P. T. Barnum to found Barnum and Bailey's Circus, later merged with Ringling Brothers.

Hiram Walker (July 4, 1816 — January 12, 1899)

Canadian distiller Hiram Walker developed Canadian Club Whiskey.

Cartooning

Rube Goldberg (July 4, 1883 — December 7, 1970)

Rube Goldberg is best known for his popular cartoon series of complex gadgets that perform simple tasks. He is the namesake of cartooning's Reuben Award, was the first president of the National Cartoonists Society, and won a Pulitzer Prize for political cartooning in 1948.

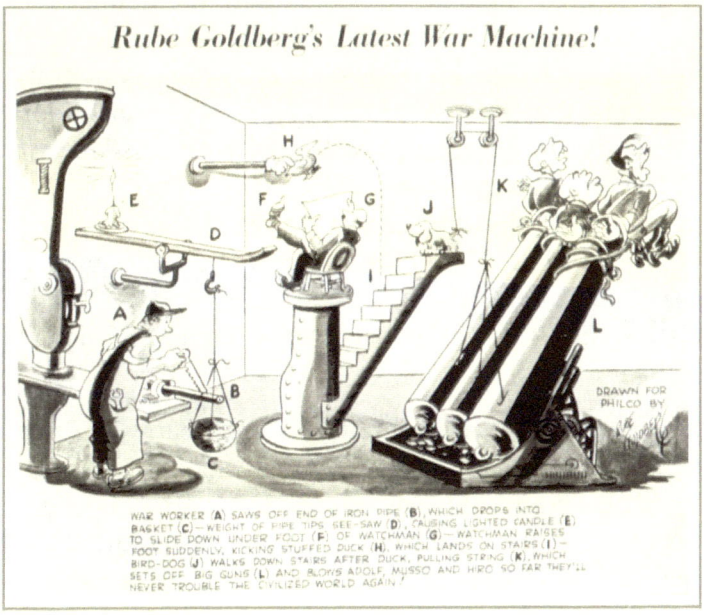

"Rube Goldberg's Latest War Machine," created for the US War Production Board

Crime and Law

Meyer Lansky
(July 4, 1902 — January 15, 1983)

Known as the "Mob's Accountant," organized crime figure Meyer Lansky (left) was a major figure in the development of the "National Crime Syndicate," building a gambling empire. He assisted the US government in anti-Nazi efforts in World War II, tried to consolidate ownership of gambling operations in Cuba. The character Hyman Roth in *The Godfather Part II* is based on Lansky, and he appears as himself in many other films and TV shows about organized crime.

Bill Tilghman (July 4, 1854 — November 1, 1924)

American Old West lawman Bill Tilghman was part of the "Dodge City Peace Commission" along with Wyatt Earp and Bat Masterson. He became deputy US marshal in Oklahoma, where he was credited with bringing law and order to the region. He was murdered in 1924 by a corrupt Prohibition agent.

Film and Television

The Situation (July 4, 1981 —)

Jersey Shore reality TV personality Michael Sorrentino is best known by his nickname "The Situation."

Max Elliott Slade (July 4, 1980 —)

As a child, Slade starred in the *3 Ninjas* film series.

Becki Newton (July 4, 1978 —)

Sitcom actress Becki Newton is best known as Amanda on *Ugly Betty* and Quinn on *How I Met Your Mother*.

Neil Morrissey (July 4, 1962 —)

English actor Neil Morrissey is the voice of Bob in *Bob the Builder* and Eddie Lawson in the BBC One series *Waterloo Road*.

Geraldo Rivera (July 4, 1943 —)

Journalist and television personality Geraldo Rivera hosted the daytime talk show *Geraldo* for 11 years and is also remembered for his 1986 syndicated special *The Mystery of Al Capone's Vault*.

Karolyn Grimes (July 4, 1940 —)

Child actress Karolyn Grimes is best known as Zuzu Bailey in the Christmas classic *It's a Wonderful Life*.

Stephen Boyd (July 4, 1931 — June 2, 1977)

Irish actor Stephen Boyd is best remembered for his role as Messala in 1959's *Ben-Hur.*

Neil Simon (July 4, 1927 —)

Playwright Neil Simon's many hits include *Barefoot in the Park, The Odd Couple,* and *Lost in Yonkers,* many of which have been made into films.

Photo: Ivo Bulanda

Gina Lollobrigida (July 4, 1927 —)

Italian actress Gina Lollobrigida (left) was a sex symbol of the 1950s and 1960s. She received a Golden Globe for *Come September* and another nomination for *Buona Sera, Mrs. Campbell.*

Eva Marie Saint (July 4, 1924 —)

Eva Marie Saint won a Best Supporting Actress Oscar for *On the Waterfront* and starred in the Alfred Hitchcock thriller *North by Northwest.*

Gloria Stuart (July 4, 1910 — September 26, 2010)

After an early screen career in which she appeared in such roles as Claude Rains' girlfriend in *The Invisible Man*, Gloria Stuart retired for many years until playing the elderly Rose Dawson Calvert in the 1997 film *Titanic*, for which she received an Academy Award nomination, the oldest person ever nominated for that honor.

Louis B Mayer (July 4, 1885* — October 29, 1957)

Producer Louis B. Mayer created the Hollywood "star system" as head of MGM. (*Mayer always gave his birthdate as July 4, 1885, but he was actually born on July 12, 1884.)

Letters

Ann Landers (July 4, 1918 — June 22, 2002)

Advice columnist Eppie Friedman Lederer took over the "Ask Ann Landers" feature at the Chicago *Sun-Times* in 1955, and turned Ann Landers into a national institution. Her twin sister Pauline also became an advice columnist, "Dear Abby."

Abigail Van Buren (July 4, 1918 — January 16, 2013)

Pauline Friedman Phillips founded the advice column "Dear Abby," using the pseudonym Abigail Van Buren. At its height, it was the most widely-syndicated newspaper column in the world. Her twin sister Eppie became "Ann Landers."

Lionel Trilling (July 4, 1905 — November 5, 1975)

Lionel Trilling is considered one of the leading American cultural critics of the 20th century.

Nathaniel Hawthorne (July 4, 1804 — May 19, 1864)

One of the first major American novelists, Nathaniel Hawthorne (left) is known for such works as *The Scarlet Letter*, *The House of the Seven Gables*, and his anthology *Twice-Told Tales*.

Military

Giuseppe Garibaldi (July 4, 1807 — June 2, 1882)

Italian general and politician Giuseppe Garibaldi was a military leader in the campaign to unify Italy, and also led campaigns in Brazil and Uruguay. He was offered a general's role in the American Civil War by Abraham Lincoln. Internationally famous, he led a major Italian political party and served in the Italian parliament.

Giuseppe Garibaldi

George Everest (July 4, 1790 — December 1, 1866)

Colonel Sir George Everest was Surveyor-General of India. Mount Everest (ཇོ་མོ་གླང་མ, pronounced "Chomolungma" in Tibetan) was named for him, despite his objections.

Music

Michael Sweet (July 4, 1943 —)

Michael Sweet was a vocalist and lead guitarist for Boston and for the Christian rock band Stryper.

Bill Withers (July 4, 1938 —)

Recording artist Bill Wither's many hits include "Lean on Me," "Ain't No Sunshine," and "Just the Two of Us."

Mitch Miller (July 4, 1911 — July 31, 2010)

Orchestra leader Mitch Miller (left, with dancers) is best remembered as the host of the 1960s television series *Sing Along with Mitch.*

Irving Caesar (July 4, 1895 — December 18, 1996)

Irving Caesar wrote the lyrics for "Swanee," "Crazy Rhythm," "Tea for Two," "Animal Crackers in My Soup," and "Just a Gigolo." He was a founder of the Songwriters Guild of America and is in the Songwriters Hall of Fame.

Stephen Foster (July 4, 1826 — January 13, 1864)

Often called the "father of American music," songwriter Stephen Foster's many well-known songs are "Oh! Susanna," "Camptown Races," "My Old Kentucky Home," and "Jeanie with the Light Brown Hair."

Sheet music for "Willie We Have Missed You" by Stephen Foster

Politics

Kathleen Kennedy Townsend (July 4, 1951 —)

Eldest child of assassinated Presidential candidate Robert F. Kennedy, Kathleen Kennedy Towson was elected Lieutenant Governor of Maryland in 1995.

Ron Kovic (July 4, 1946 —)

Paralyzed in the Vietnam War, Ron Kovic authored the memoir *Born on the Fourth of July*, made into an Oliver Stone film starring Tom Cruse. His story was the inspiration for the Jane Fonda film *Coming Home*.

George Murphy (July 4, 1902 — May 3, 1992)

A musical star in the *Broadway Melody* films and many others, George Murphy became the first notable US actor to make the transition from movies to politics when he was elected US Senator from California in 1965.

Calvin Coolidge (July 4, 1872 — January 5, 1933)

Calvin Coolidge was the 30th President of the United States. Nicknamed "Silent Cal," he was known for saying very little. "I think the American people want a solemn ass as President," he said, "and I think I will go along with them."

Calvin Coolidge

Science

Henrietta Swan Leavitt (July 4, 1868 — December 12, 1921)

Astronomer Henrietta Leavitt discovered the relationship between the luminosity and period of Cepheid variable stars, which allowed astronomers to measure the distance between Earth and other galaxies, and later helped prove that the universe is expanding.

Sports

La'Roi Glover (July 4, 1974 —)

During his 13-year NFL career, tackle La'Roi Glover was a four-time All-Pro selection.

Todd Marinovich (July 4, 1969 —)

As a high school athlete, Todd Marinovich was featured in a Sports Illustrated article, "Bred to be a Superstar." His career derailed from marijuana use.

Harvey and Horace Grant (July 4, 1965 —)

Twin brothers Horace and Harvey Grant both played in the NBA.

Henri Leconte (July 4, 1963 —)

French tennis player Henri Leconte helped France win the 1991 Davis Cup, and ranked as high as #5 in the world.

Barry Windham (July 4, 1960 —)

Wrester Barry Windham is in the WWE Hall of Fame as a member of the Four Horsemen.

Sid Vicious (July 4, 1960 —)

WWF/WWE multiple world champion Sid Eudy wrestled under a variety of ring names.

Morganna (July 4, 1947 —)

Burlesque artist Morganna (right) became known as "the Kissing Bandit" for rushing onto the field during baseball and other sports games and kissing the players.

Andre Spitzer (July 4, 1945 — September 6, 1972)

Fencing master and coach of the 1972 Israeli Summer Olympics team, Andre Spitzer was one of 11 athletes and coaches killed in the Munich massacre.

Emerson Boozer (July 4, 1943 —)

Emerson Boozer is in the College Football Hall of Fame for his years at Maryland State College, and played for the New York Jets as a pro.

Floyd Little (July 4, 1942 —)

Pro Football Hall of Fame quarterback Floyd Little was known as "the Franchise" during his time with the Denver Broncos.

Hal Lanier (July 4, 1942 —)

Hal Lanier played for the San Francisco Giants and the New York Yankees from 1964 through 1973, and subsequently managed the Houston Astros.

John Sterling (July 4, 1938 —)

Sportscaster John Sterling has announced every.Yankees game since 1989.

George Steinbrenner (July 4, 1930 — July 13, 2010)

Outspoken and controversial owner of the New York Yankees, George Steinbrenner (left) was also involved in Great Lakes shipping.

Bill Tuttle (July 4, 1929 — July 27, 1998)

Center fielder Bill Tuttle became a public speaker about the dangers of chewing tobacco after contracting oral cancer.

Al Davis (July 4, 1929 — October 8, 2011)

General manager and head coach Al Davis became principal owner of the Oakland Raiders in 1972. He was the AFL Commissioner in 1966 at the time of the NFL/AFL merger.

Peter Angelos (July 4, 1929 —)

Attorney Peter Angelos is majority owner of the Baltimore Orioles.

Chuck Tanner (July 4, 1928 — February 11, 2011)

As a left fielder, Tanner played for eight seasons for four different teams, then became a manager , most notably coaching Pittsburgh to the 1979 World Series championship.

Johnnie Parsons (July 4, 1918 — September 8, 1984)

Indianapolis 500 champion for 1950, Johnnie Parsons is the only Indy 500 winner to have his name misspelled on the trophy.

Manolete (July 4, 1917 — August 29, 1947)

Considered by some to be the greatest bullfighter of all time, Manolete's death in the ring in 1947 led to three days of national mourning in Spain.

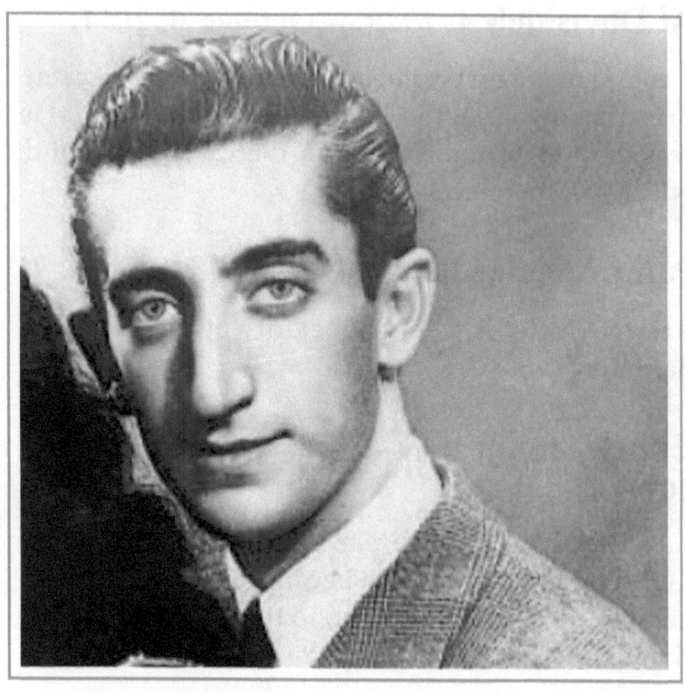

Manolete

Who Died on July 4?

Art and Illustration

Bob Ross (October 29, 1942 — July 4, 1995)
Painter and art instructor Bob Ross hosted the long-running PBS series *The Joy of Painting*.

Art Sansom (September 16, 1920 — July 4, 1991)
American cartoonist Art Sansom is best known for the long-running newspaper strip *The Born Loser*.

Barnett Newman (January 29, 1905 — July 4, 1970)
American abstract expressionist painter Barnett Newman is considered one of the most important color field painters.

Film and Television

Charles Kuralt (September 10, 1934 — July 4, 1997)

Television journalist Charles Kuralt is best known for his "On the Road" segments on *The CBS Evening News with Walter Cronkite* and as the anchor of *CBS News Sunday Morning*.

Eva Gabor (February 11, 1919 — July 4, 1995)

Actress Eva Gabor is best remembered for her role on the TV sitcom *Green Acres*.

Eva Gabor (right) with Eddie Albert from *Green Acres*

Letters

Georgette Heyer (August 16, 1902 — July 4, 1974)

British author Georgette Heyer is best known for her historical Regency romances and for her detective and thriller novels.

August Derleth (February 24, 1909 — July 4, 1971)

Publisher and horror writer August Derleth founded Arkham House, which first published the writings of H. P. Lovecraft, and wrote numerous books, both supernatural fiction and in other genres.

Monteiro Lobato (April 18, 1882 — July 4, 1948)

Monteiro Lobato is one of Brazil's most influential writers of books both for children and adults.

Alan Seeger (June 22, 1888 — July 4, 1916)

American poet Alan Seeger is best known for "I Have a Rendezvous with Death," a favorite poem of John F. Kennedy. He is the uncle of folk singer Pete Seeger and was a classmate of T. S. Eliot at Harvard. He died in the World War I Battle of the Somme as a member of the French Foreign Legion.

François-René de Chateaubriand
(September 4, 1768 — July 4, 1848)

French author Chateaubriand is considered the founder of French Romanticism in literature.

Samuel Richardson **(August 19, 1689 — July 4, 1761)**

English writer Samuel Richardson's best known work is *Pamela: Or, Virtue Rewarded*, first published in 1740.

Military and Exploration

Benjamin O. Davis, Jr. **(February 11, 1919 — July 4, 1995)**

African-American USAF officer Benjamin O. Davis, Jr., (next page) commanded the World War II 99th and 32nd Fighter Groups, known as the Tuskegee Airmen, and subsequently became a four-star USAF general, following in the footsteps of his father, Benjamin O. Davis, Sr., the first African-American general in US Army history.

Lothar von Richthofen **(September 27, 1894 — July 4, 1922)**

World War I German fighter ace Lothar von Richthofen scored 40 victories. He was the younger brother of Manfred von Richthofen, better known as the Red Baron.

World War II promotional cartoon of Benjamin O. Davis, Jr.

Pedro Teixeira (unknown — July 4, 1641)

Portuguese explorder Pedro Teixeira was the first European to travel the entire length of the Amazon.

Hayreddin Barbarossa (c. 1478 — July 4, 1546)

Admiral of the Fleet for the Ottoman Empire, Pasha Hayreddin Barbarossa's naval victories allowed the Ottomans to dominate the Mediterranean until the Battle of Lepanto in 1571.

Pedro de Alvarado (c. 1485 or 1495 — July 4, 1541)

Conquistador of most of Central America, Pedro de Alvarado was renowned as a soldier but infamous for mass murders of indigenous people.

Raynald of Châtillon (c. 1125 — July 4, 1187)

Raynald was a controversial knight of the Second Crusade, accused of numerous atrocities and oath breaking. He was defeated by صلاح الدين يوسف بن أيوب (Saladin) who had him executed.

Music

Barry White (September 12, 1944 — July 4, 2003)

Two-time Grammy winner Barry White (left) was known for his distinctive bass voice and romantic image. His two biggest hits were, "You're the First, the Last, My Everything," and "Can't Get Enough of Your Love, Babe."

Politics

Jesse Helms (October 18, 1921 — July 4, 2008)

Jesse Helms was a five-term Republican senator from North Carolina. He was known as "Senator No" for his opposition to civil rights, integration, disability rights, and gay rights.

Hannibal Hamlin (August 27, 1809 — July 4, 1891)

Hannibal Hamlin was Vice President of the United States during Abraham Lincoln's first term as President.

James Monroe (April 28, 1758 — July 4, 1831)

Fifth President of the United States James Monroe (right) was the last person to hold that office who had been a Founding Father of the United States and the third to die on July 4.

John Adams (October 30, 1735 [O.S. October 19, 1735] — July 4, 1826)

American Founding Father John Adams was first Vice President and second President of the United States. He died on the same day as Thomas Jefferson. (*For an explanation of "O.S.," see "On Dates" in the Copyrights and Credits section of this book.)

Thomas Jefferson (April 13, 1743 [O.S. April 2, 1743] — July 4, 1761)

American Founding Father Thomas Jefferson was principal author of the Declaration of Independence and third President of the United States. He died on the same day as John Adams.

Religion

Swami Vivekananda (January 12, 1863 — July 4, 1902)

Swami Vivekananda was a major force in the 19th century revival of Hinduism in India, and is credited with introducing Vedanta and Yoga to the western world. In India, his birthday is celebrated as National Youth Day.

Joseph Brackett (May 6, 1797 — July 4, 1882)

Shaker elder Joseph Brackett is known as the composer of "Simple Gifts." The melody was famously incorporated in the 1944 Aaron Copeland composition *Appalachian Spring*.

Saint Ulrich of Augsburg (c. 890 — July 4, 973)

Bishop of Augsburg, Ulrich was the first saint to be officially canonized by the Vatican rather than proclaimed a saint by public accord.

Saint Ulrich of Augsburg by Anton Cebej

Science

Marie Curie (November 7, 1867 — July 4, 1934)

Polish physicist and chemist Marie Skłodowska Curie (left) was the first woman to win a Nobel Prize, the only woman to win the Nobel Prize in two categories, and the only person to win the Nobel in multiple sciences. She discovered the elements polonium and radium.

Giovanni Schiaparelli (March 14, 1835 — July 4, 1910)

Italian astronomer Giovanni Schiaparelli is known for his telescopic observations of Mars, in which he identified a network of linear structures on the surface of the Red Planet. He described them as *canali* (channels) in Italian, which was subsequently mistranslated as "canals" in English, giving rise to the false idea of intelligent life on Mars.

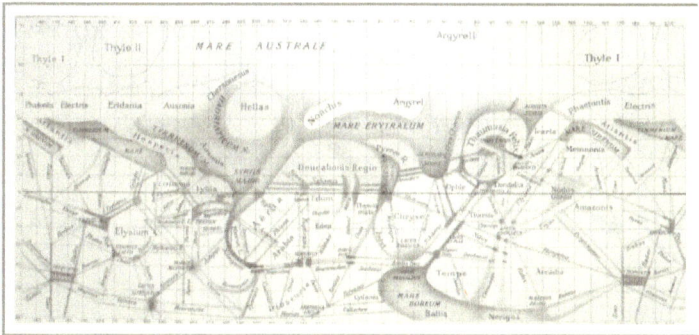

A map of Mars drawn by Giovannie Schiaparelli, 1890

William Kirby (September 19, 1759 — July 4, 1850)

William Kirby is considered the "founder of entomology."

Sports

Jimmy Bivins (December 16, 1919 — July 4, 2012)

Although he was denied a shot at the title, boxer Jimmy Bivins defeated eight of the eleven world champions he faced in his career. He was inducted into the International Boxing Hall of Fame in 1999.

Scamper (1977 — July 4, 2012)

American Quarter Horse Scamper was inducted into the Pro Rodeo Hall of Fame. He was cloned by genetics company Viagen.

Hank Stram (January 3, 1923 — July 4, 2005)

Football coach Hank Stram led the Kansas City Chiefs for 15 years. He was inducted into the Pro Football Hall of Fame in 2003.

Adrian Adonis (September 12, 1954 — July 4, 1988)

American professional wrestler Keith Franke was best known by his ring name, "Adorable" Adrian Adonis.

Suzanne Lenglen (May 24, 1899 — July 4, 1938)

French tennis player Suzanne Lenglen won 31 championship titles between 1914 and 1926, becoming the first female tennis celebrity. She was nicknamed *La Divine* by the French press.

Suzanne Lenglen playing, 1920

July
The Seventh Month

"Here men from the planet Earth first set foot upon the Moon. July 1969 AD."

— Plaque left on the site of the Apollo 11 landing.

In the original Roman calendar, the month of July was named *Quintilis*, the fifth month, because the Romans originally counted the first of March as the beginning of the new year.

Quintilis was renamed July by the Roman senate in honor of Gaius Julius Caesar after his death in 44 BCE, because Caesar, among his other accomplishments, had undertaken a major calendar reform, known as the Julian calendar, which remained the standard European calendar until 1582 CE. (Not to be outdone, Emperor Augustus arranged for the next month, Sextilis, to be renamed in *his* honor.)

July is one of the seven months with 31 days. In a common (non-leap) year, it always starts on the same day of the week as April, and on the same day of the week as January in leap years. Strangely, in common years, no other month of the year ends on the same day of the week as July! (In leap years, the last day of July and January fall on the same day.)

July in Other Cultures

In Latin, the month of July was spelled *Iulius,* as the Romans did not have the letter "J."

In Albanian, the month is *korrik*. Arabs call the month يوليه (yūlia).

It is юли (juli) in Bulgaria, *lipanj* in Croatia, and *červen* in Czech.

The Finns call the month *kesäkuu* and the Greeks call it Ιούλιος (Ioúlios).

There is a Hebrew calendar, but when they refer to the Gregorian month, it's יולי (yûlî).

In Gaelic, July is *Meitheamh mi an Mheitheamh*, and in Russian, it is июнь (ijun').

The Chinese use 六月 (liùyuè in Mandarin);

Koreans 유월 (yuweol); and it's 腩鞋 (tháng sáu) in Vietnamese

July Superstitions

- "Those who in July do wed, must labor for their daily bread."
- The corn harvest will be good if the corn growing in the fields is "knee high by the Fourth of July."
- "If the first of July be rainy weather, 'twill rain more or less for four weeks together."
- "Rain or dry, plant your turnips on the Fourth of July."

July Symbols

Birthstone: Ruby
(symbolizes success, devotion, and integrity.

Birth Flowers: Water Lily (purity of heart) or Larkspur (lightness and levity.)

Birth Tree: Elm (strength of will and intuition).

"Labors of the Month: July," by Simon Bening

July Events

Honorary Months

Presidents, Congresses, and nations around the world issue proclamations recognizing particular months to honor certain causes. These events generally fall in July.

- Eye Injury Prevention Month
- International Massage Week
- UV Safety Month

Moveable and Multi-Day Events

Some events take place over a specific week or time period. Start and finish dates may vary from year to year. Some events occur on different days each year (such as "fourth Saturday of a month").

Fireworks Safety Month (United States)

Fireworks Safety Month in the United States runs from June 1 through July 4 each year.

Sobriety Checkpoint Week (United States)

National Sobriety Checkpoint Week runs from June 30 through July 4 each year.

Tooth Filing Ceremonies (Bali)

In Balinese popular beliefs, having your teeth filed during the months of July and August helps rid you of the invisible forces of evil. The ceremony, known as *Mepandes*, has been practiced for over 2,000 years.

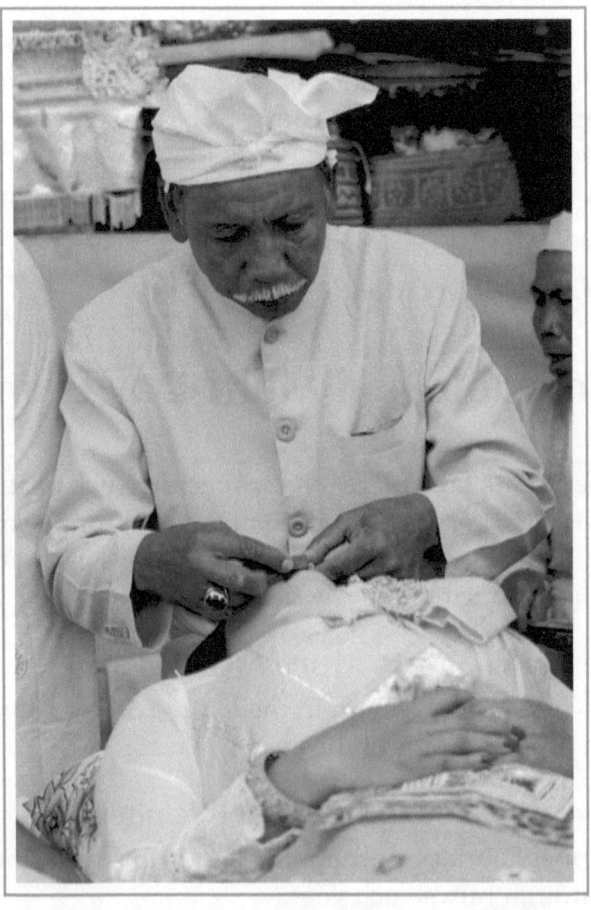

Mepandes ceremony (Photo: Abdes Prestaka)

July Zodiac Signs

From the perspective of someone on Earth, the Sun appears to move through the sky throughout the year, along a path astronomers call the ecliptic plane. The ecliptic plane is divided into twelve constellations, known as the zodiac, based on traditionally observed patterns of stars. On your birthday, you can't see your constellation, because it's part of the daytime sky.

The zodiac was first developed by Babylonian astronomers about 2,500 years ago. Because they were unaware that the Earth wobbles like a spinning top (a motion known as *precession*), they didn't make allowance for the fact that the Sun's path through the zodiac changes over time.

That means there are now two sets of dates for your birth sign. The *tropical* dates are the original Babylonian dates; the *siderial* dates tell you where the Sun actually appears as it moves along its annual path.

In tropical reckoning, July 4 is in Cancer, and in siderial reckoning, July 4 is in Gemini.

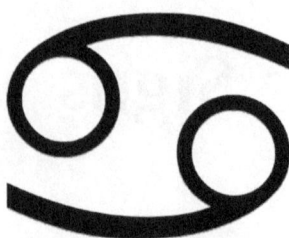

Cancer

Tropical June 21 to July 22
Siderial July 16 to August 15

The Greek word for "crab" is Καρκινος (Karkinos), later Latinized as *carcinus,* which evolved into our word *cancer.* In Greek mythology. In one telling, when Hercules was battling the Hydra, Zeus's wife Hera sent Karkinos to distract the hero, but Hercules kicked it with such force that it was thrown into the sky, becoming a constellation. (Some say that Hercules crushed the crab with his foot and that Hera placed the crab in the night sky as a reward for its service.)

Because of the association with the disease, some astrologers refer to those born under the sign of Cancer as "moon children," because the ruling planet of Cancer is the Moon.

Cancers (or Moon Children) are supposed to be loyal, dependable, caring, and adaptable, but can also be moody, self-pitying, and oversensitive. Cancers are supposed to be particularly compatible with Scorpios, Piceans, and other Cancers.

Gemini

Tropical May 22 to June 21

Siderial June 16 to July 15

In Greek and Roman mythology, Castor and Pollux were twin brothers, both born to Leda. Castor, however, was a mortal, son of the King of Sparta, whereas Pollux was the son of Zeus, who had seduced (or raped) Leda while disguised as a swan. When Castor was killed, Pollux asked to share his divine immortality with his brother, and so Zeus transformed them both into the constellation of Gemini.

In astrology, Gemini is considered a masculine and air sign, ruled by Mercury. Geminis are supposed to be flexible, responsive, and sociable. Positive traits include intelligence and independence; negative traits include impatience and impulsiveness. Geminis are supposed to be particularly compatible with Aquarians, Libras, and other Geminis.

Illustration by Edward Penfield

What Day of the Week is July 4?

On what day of the week does July 4 fall?

Surprisingly, this isn't an easy question. Because the calendar year is 365 days long (366 in leap years), it doesn't divide evenly by the seven days of the week.

Also, the Earth goes around the Sun in about 365-1/4 days, so a calendar tends to drift over time. That's why the same date falls on different weekdays in different years.

This is made even more complicated by a change in calendars that took place in 1582. Our modern calendar has its roots in ancient Rome, in a calendar reform conducted by Julius Caesar. Caesar commissioned mathematicians to attack the problem, and they came up with the idea of *leap years*, and thus standardized the calendar for centuries to come. This was called the *Julian calendar*.

Over time, however, the small errors in Caesar's calculation compounded. That's why Pope Gregory XIII commissioned the *Gregorian calendar*, used in most of the world today. Some countries converted in 1582, when the calendar was first developed; some converted later; other still haven't changed.

Gregorian and Julian aren't the only types of calendars. The Hebrew year, the Islamic year, and many other calendars are used in different parts of the world and among different people.

You can convert Gregorian dates to other calendars, including the Hebrew calendar, the Islamic calendar, and even the Mayan calendar by visiting the Fourmilab Calendar Converter at http://www.fourmilab.ch/documents/calendar/.

Chinese calendar systems are quite complex and have changed several times; a full discussion is far beyond the scope of this book. If you're interested, you can find information here: http://www.hermetic.ch/cal_stud/chinese_cal.htm.

A 50-year brass perpetual calendar.

Copyright, Credit, and Contact

Follow Us

Our blog *Dobson's Improbable History* (http://improbhistory.blogspot.com) features short articles on events and people associated with each day, and updates several times each week. You can also get a daily "What Happened In History" message and all the latest Timespinner Press news by following us on Facebook at https://www.facebook.com/TimespinnerPress. Our Twitter feed @SidewiseThinker links you to all our News of the Day.

Contact Us

Find an error or a format problem? Want information about the series, about us, or about when the volume for your special day might be available? Please email us at editor@timespinnerpress.com. (We also take requests if your special day isn't yet complete. Please give us at least six weeks' notice if possible.)

On Dates

Historians use "CE" (Common Era) and "BCE" (Before the Common Era) instead of the more common "AD" (*Anno Domini,* or Year of Our Lord) and "BC" (Before Christ), reflecting the fact that the year-numbering system established by the Gregorian calendar is used throughout the world in many countries not culturally Christian.

The CE/BCE designation dates back to at least 1708, and has been adopted as a standard by the United Nations and the Universal Postal Union. Because this series of books covers events and people of all nations and cultures, we use the CE/BCE terms.

The abbreviation "O.S." ("Old Style") on some dates refers to the fact that the Russian Empire did not switch from the Julian to the Gregorian calendar at the same time as the rest of Europe, and therefore some figures and events have two dates. (See "What Day of the Week…" for an explanation of Julian and Gregorian dates.)

People and events whose original names are not in the Western alphabet have their native names (where possible) in the appropriate script shown in parenthesis. If you are using an e-reader to access an electronic version of this book, all characters don't always display on all devices.

Sources and Art Credits

We owe a great debt to Wikipedia, which is our first stop for research. We attempt to make independent confirmation of all important dates and facts through a variety of other sources. Other sources we frequently use include the Library of Congress; "on this day" listings from *Encyclopedia Britannica*, the New York *Times*, and the BBC; and, of course, the always essential Google.

All art and photographs are either in the public domain, used under a Creative Commons license, or with a "fair use" justification, and most frequently come from Wikimedia Commons and the Library of Congress Prints and Photographs Division.

Attribution is provided where requested by the copyright owner or when of historical significance, listed below. For information about any particular illustration or photograph, please contact us.

- The cover photograph of a Fourth of July fireworks display at the Washington Monument was taken in 1986 by SSGT Lono Kollars of the US Air Force. It is in the public domain as a work of the US federal government.

- The illustration of the month of July used on the back cover and as the frontispiece is from the French Gothic illuminated manuscript *Les Très Riches Heures du duc de Berry* by the Limbourg Brothers, Jean Colombe, and an intermediate painter whose name is lost to history. It is in the public domain because its copyright has expired.

- The photograph of the US Declaration of Independence is in the public domain as a work of the US government.

- The 1900 painting, "Writing the Declaration of Independence, 1776," is a work by Jean Leon Gerome Ferris. The original is in the collection of the Virginia Historical Society and the image is from the Library of Congress Prints and Photographs Division. It is in the public domain because its copyright has expired.

- The NASA/ESA Hubble Space Telescope photograph of the Crab Nebula is in the public domain as a work created by the National Aeronautics and Space Administration and the European Space Agency.

- The 1772 portrait of George Washington by Charles Wilson Peale is in the public domain because its copyright has expired. It is part of the Washington-Custis-Lee Collection at Washington and Lee University, Lexington, Virginia.

- The 1839 engraving of the Erie Canal is by W. H. Bartlett, and is in the public domain because its copyright has expired.

- The illustration by John Tenniel from Alice's Adventures in Wonderland was first published in 1865. It is in the public domain because its copyright has expired.

- The photograph of boxer Jack Johnson was taken between 1910 and 1915, and is in the public domain because its copyright has expired. The image is from the George Grantham Bain Collection, Library of Congress Prints and Photographs Division.

- The 1937 photograph of Lou Gehrig was cropped from a larger picture. It is from the Harris & Ewing Collection, Library of Congress Prints and Photographs Division. There are no known restrictions on the use of items from the collection.

- The photograph of the Pathfinder rover on Mars was taken by the lander. The image is in the public domain as a work of NASA.

- The 1895 lithograph of James Bailey is in the public domain because its copyright has expired.

- The cartoon "Rube Goldberg's Latest War Machine" was created for the US Office for Emergency Management, War Production Board, between 1942 and 1943, and is in the public domain as a work created for the US federal government. The original is in the collection of the National Archives and Records Administration, Special Media Archives Services Division.

- The 1958 photograph of Meyer Lansky is from the New York *World-Telegram & Sun Collection*, donated to the Library of Congress Prints and Photographs Division. It was deeded to the public domain by the donor as part of the Instrument of Gift.

- The photograph of Gina Lollobrigida is by Ivo Bulanda, retouched by César, and is used here under CC-BY-SA 3.0.

- The photograph of Nathaniel Hawthorne is by acclaimed photographer Mathew Brady. It is from the Brady-Handy Collection of the Library of Congress Prints and Photographs Division, and is in the public domain because its copyright has expired.

- The photographer of the 1886 portrait of Giuseppe Garibaldi is unknown. The image in the public domain because its copyright has expired.

- The 1961 NBC publicity photograph of Mitch Miller from the TV show *Sing Along With Mitch* is in the public domain because it was first published in the US between 1923 and 1977 without a copyright notice.

- The 1854 sheet music cover from Stephen Foster's "Willie We Have Missed You" is in the public domain because its copyright has expired.

- The 1919 photograph of Calvin Coolidge as Governor of Massachusetts is in the collection of the Library of Congress Prints and Photographs Division. It is in the public domain because its copyright has expired.

- The advertisement for Morganna' appearance at Champ's night club appeared in the Montreal *Gazette*, January 27, 1969. The copyright status of the advertisement is unknown. It is used here under "free use" rationale because it illustrates the historically significant person in question, no free image can be found to replace it, and it is used at a low resolution and small size unsuitable for the production of counterfeit goods.

- The 2008 photograph of George Steinbrenner was released into the public domain by the New York Yankees and Major League Baseball, as well as by its Internet host, Archive.org. It is a clip from a 2010 film produced by MLB looking at Steinbrenner's life and work.

- The 1947 photograph of Manolete is used here under CC-BY-SA 3.0. It has been cropped from the original, which shows him with Lupe Sino.

- The 1965 NBC publicity photograph of Eddie Albert and Eva Gabor from *Green Acres* is in the public domain because it was first published in the US between 1923 and 1977 without a copyright notice.

- The biographical cartoon of Benjamin O. Davis, Jr., was created by Charles Henry Alston in 1943 for the Office of War Information's News Bureau, and is now in the collection of the National Archives and Records Administration. It is in the public domain as a work created by the US federal government.

- The photograph of Barry White was taken by "King William" and is used here under CC-BY-SA 3.0.

- The official White House portrait of James Monroe was painted c. 1819 by Samuel Morse, and is in the public domain because its copyright has expired.

- The 1765 painting of Saint Ulrich of Augsburg is by Anton Cebej, and is in the collection of the National Gallery of Slovenia. It is in the public domain because its copyright has expired.

- The 1911 photograph of Marie Curie is in the public domain because its copyright has expired. The name of the photographer is unknown.

- The 1890 map of Mars by Giovannie Schiaparelli is in the public domain because its copyright has expired.

- The 1920 photograph of Suzanne Lenglen at the French tennis championships was by Agence de presse Meurisse and is now in the collection of the Bibliothèque nationale de France. It is in the public domain because its copyright has expired.

- The photograph of a ruby was released into the public domain by its creator.

- The photograph of a water lily at Kew Gardens was taken by "Dinkum," who released it into the public domain under the CC0 1.0 dedication.

- The engraving of parts of the American elm (*ulmus americana*) was taken from The American Cyclopaedia, published in 1879. It is in the public domain because its copyright has expired.

- The illustration "Labors of the Months: July" by Simon Bening is from a Flemish Book of Hours published in the first half of the 16th century. It is in the public domain because its copyright has expired.

- The photograph of the Mepandes tooth-filing ceremony was taken in 2009 by Abdes Prestaka, and is used here under the CC-BY-SA 2.0 license.

- The photograph of the 1906 automobile calendar by Edward Penfield is from the Library of Congress Prints and Photographs Division, and is in the public domain because it was published prior to January 1, 1923.

- The 50-year perpetual calendar photograph is in the public domain.

License Description and Terms

Aside from material purely in the public domain, photographs and other material in this book are used under specific licenses permitting free use, usually with attribution. For full text and terms of these licenses, click or enter the appropriate links below.

- Creative Commons Attribution 2.0 Generic (CC-BY 2.0): http://creativecommons.org/licenses/by/2.0/deed.en

- Creative Commons Attribution-Share Alike 3.0 Generic (CC-BY-SA 3.0): http://creativecommons.org/licenses/by-sa/3.0/

- Creative Commons Attribution-Share Alike 2.5 Generic (CC-BY-SA 2.5): http://creativecommons.org/licenses/by-sa/2.5/deed.en

- Creative Commons Attribution-Share Alike 2.0 Generic (CC-BY-SA 2.0): http://creativecommons.org/licenses/by/2.0/deed.en http://creativecommons.org/publicdomain/zero/1.0/deed.en

- Creative Commons Attribution-Share Alike 1.0 Generic (CC-BY-SA 1.0): http://creativecommons.org/licenses/by-sa/1.0/deed.en

- CC0 1.0 Universal (CC0 1.0) Public Domain Dedication (CC0 1.0)

- GNU Free Documentation License (GFDL): http://en.wikipedia.org/wiki/Wikipedia:Text_of_the_GNU_Free_Documentation_License

Timespinner
Press